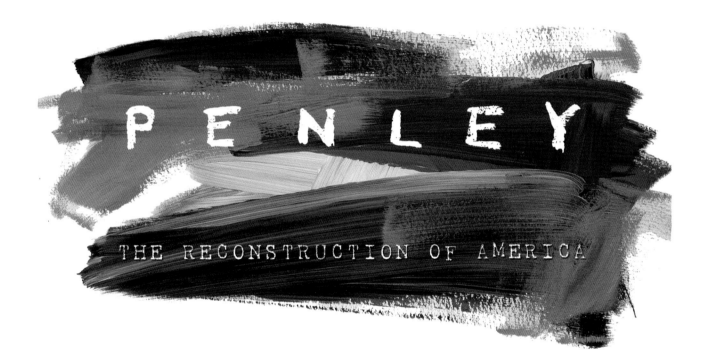

PENLEY

THE RECONSTRUCTION OF AMERICA

FOR BOB, YOU CREATED
A FRANKENSTEIN.

MERCER

Published by
Mercer University Press
1400 Coleman Avenue
Macon, Georgia 31207
MUP/H778

First printing

Edited by Matt Carrothers

Library of Congress Cataloging-in-Publication Data

Penley, Steve, 1964-
The reconstruction of America / Steve Penley—1st ed.
p. cm.
ISBN-13: 978-0-88146-139-8 (hardback : alk. paper)
ISBN-10: 0-88146-139-3 (hardback : alk. paper)
1. Penley, Steve, 1964—Catalogs.
2. Americana in art—Catalogs.
I. Title.
ND237.P355A4 2008
759.13—dc22

2008030508

Book and jacket design by Burtch Hunter Design / www.burtchhunter.com

PENLEY

THE RECONSTRUCTION OF AMERICA

We spend so much time looking toward the future, sometimes we forget about the valuable lessons of the past, and the valuable images too. Thank goodness my friend Steve Penley does not.

Steve sees what sometimes we do not, and honors what so many of our politicians will not: our history, our greatness, our very heritage. But unlike mere historians, Steve literally paints the image and reinforces the moment. It's a moment, actually many moments, we should hold dear because our history is dear, and these images even more so.

They are our memories—but what's more important, and what Steve captures so brilliantly, they are a colorful testament to our very character. In a day and age when we capture moments in snippets, Steve harkens us back to a time when we lingered longer and delved deeper.

I cannot think of a better time for this book, and Steve's message. In a world that's made kicking the United States a sport, and a media that all but shouts out the plays, it's refreshing to see Steve remembering when we were in the game, and all rooting for the same team. Our team. Our country. Our pride. Our liberty and freedom, beacon and hope.

Steve refuses to see the America that gets lectured, but the America that gets it, period. Not the America that gets roundly ripped, but the America that profoundly led. He harkens us back to when we were a shining city, and we were proud to proclaim it, not the media pap today that seems only embarrassed by it.

What Steve paints is a vivid picture, not just of what we were, but what we are. Like that old athlete who's put on a few pounds and maybe lost his way, Steve is there to say the athlete still has it, the fire is still there, and the passion still thrives. But the athlete lives in a world of other beaten-down athletes, and a carping literati that insist his best days aren't only behind him, but far worse days lie in front of him.

Steve is not so cynical, or jaded. And neither were our greatest leaders. Ronald Reagan spoke of that shining city on a hill. Abraham Lincoln talked of the "sum of our goodness." And not even half a century ago, John Kennedy reminded the world we would bear "any burden."

All this wasn't all that long ago—when we could challenge ourselves to put a man on the moon and hope in our hearts. This is the uniquely American dream. This is what made America the envy of the world, and the beacon to the world. It's why they still come in rickety rafts to be here. I have yet to see anyone, *anyone*, taking those same rafts to France, or any country that has felt free to second-guess us than remember us, and remember all we did, and do, for the world.

This is the country that helped save a planet—twice—that liberated more people than any country in the history of man; that secured freedoms for women once tortured in Iraq and quiet hope even now for freedom-seekers in Iran.

You don't hear of their triumphs; you only hear of our ills. You don't hear of the fruit of our blood-stained efforts, just the stain of blood. Rarely do we hear what's been wrought from that blood—the schools built, the hospitals opened, the shops and businesses and everyday acts of commerce reinvigorated and freedoms restored. We spend an inordinate time in this country, and outside this country, dismissing this country, even trashing this country.

This is the same country that provided hope for those who anywhere else would be considered hopeless. There aren't too many countries that would provide the opportunity for a ruffian wayward New Jersey kid to become a star named Sinatra, or another from a broken Arkansas home, a U.S. President.

That doesn't happen elsewhere. It happens here. Again and again. We're called a melting pot, not so much for the variety of people and backgrounds in our mix, but the bubbling up of opportunities at our disposal. That is our essence. This is our broth. And Steve Penley is our chef.

And in this book, Steve also is our guide—not only to our past but the very recipe for our greatness.

Sometimes we forget the recipe, but I suspect, like my Italian grandmother, we've memorized the ingredients. Steve has captured those ingredients and shown us what we all cannot and should not forget. The true majesty of our country is defined not by the big things we do, but the little things we cherish, and the precious images and moments we cherish more.

I have yet to run into anyone at a funeral who recounts how the deceased was moved by international events, but tiny ones. Not by her brush with fame, but her contact with kids, or friends, the neighborhood church, or the local food kitchen. We remember not great acts, but small ones—the letter when we were sick, the call when we were down, the smile when we were anxious.

I'm not saying we Americans solely possess these qualities. I am saying that we uniquely and proudly build on them, like no other people this world has known. We have so much for which to be grateful, and so many to whom we should always be thankful. In a day and age where we're beaten down to think we don't matter, *this* matters, and *this* book matters, and *Steve* matters.

He illustrates what we were by reminding us what we are. This isn't a book that takes us to the past. I like to think it's Steve's way of guiding us into the future. There is a difference. We could look back and say, never again, or look forward and insist, "yes, time and again."

I remember talk not too long ago when Tom Brokaw's *The Greatest Generation* was released, that this great group of men and women who survived the Great Depression and a major World War, would never be rivaled. This was my parents' generation, rapidly leaving us, but I thought then, as I do now, and I hope and pray now, not forgotten by the rest of us.

Because I'm reminded of that generation every time I reflect on my own coverage of the September 11 attacks on this country. I remember quite well going down to lower Manhattan at the time to see thousands of people fleeing those towers. Then I remember something else—dozens of rescue workers going *in* to those towers—most, maybe all, never to be heard from again.

They didn't pause, or wince, or think twice. They just charged in. And they never got out. And I thought, these are the sons and daughters, the grandsons and granddaughters of that Greatest Generation, reminding us all over again that such greatness is in our blood. It's in our very DNA. It's who we are.

Steve gets that, shows that, tells that. I just hope we never forget that.

Neil Cavuto
Fox News

"If we ever forget that we are one nation under God, then we are a nation gone under"

Ronald Wilson Reagan

PENLEY

This is my story of America, her heroes and her icons, from the revolutionary war and the founding of our nation to her rise to be the most powerful nation on Earth. This is a story of unapologetic bias towards the fact that America is Great. America is proof that no idea or dream is unattainable by free people.

In the history of civilization, the United States is the greatest nation of them all. What have we done differently over the past two hundred years? Why are we now being taught to distrust the things that have made America great? Why do so many Americans want to believe that our best days are behind us?

Our founders were optimists pursuing their dreams in a new land which was set apart from the old cultures and traditions of the world. These men sent a message to America and the world; happiness and success are not products of the government, but of the individual. The divine part of human nature stepped in during our founding. Faith in our creator has sustained us through war and peace, and that faith is our only hope in the future.

America made everything new. Our founders broke the chains of the past and created a new path. These were self reliant men who laid the foundation for a self reliant nation. When we are challenged we will always prevail.

IN AMERICA, ONLY

GOD IS OUR KING.

IN AMERICA, We look for leaders who will inspire us and our children to keep the flame of freedom alive and help fend off enemies abroad. We are secure in the knowledge that the Oval Office is not reserved for the sons and daughters of privilege, but for seemingly ordinary people with extraordinary vision. They take on personas that we project on them, but no man can live up to our expectations. I prefer to see the good.

WASHINGTON chose the title "Mr. President" because he felt it was a "common" term. He did not want the President or the office to evoke thoughts or ideas of a king set apart from its citizens. No American icon has a legacy more omnipresent than Washington. He defines the word hero. As a General He led a ragged band of soldiers to victory

against the greatest fighting force in the world. He also fought a war of public opinion. He battled a congress that was growing weary of war. Much of America was still loyal to the King. Against all odds he prevailed.

...TION

PENLEY

Jefferson viewed government as a necessary evil because he knew the abuses that would be possible in the future. Our first Presidents had uncommon wisdom. Jefferson would probably be heart broken to see government becoming so obtrusive in our lives.

Few leaders loom larger in history than Abraham Lincoln. He made us believe in the promise of America, that even the penniless sons of the frontier are at times called to save a nation. He was determined to save the union at any cost and to do this he knew that the promise of freedom must be available to all men. He recognized the fact that America could never survive unless the evil of slavery was abolished.

Presidents lose their individuality as soon as they are sworn in. They become figureheads and are subject to the portait that the media of the day paints of them. Only the perspective of history can fairly judge these men. The great Presidents transcend their individual self and become almost mythic.

TEDDY was the ultimate rugged individualist.

He was a proponent of "the strenuous life." Teddy symbolized the toughness of America. He knew that to succeed in life we have to push ourselves to be our best, and that spirit has made America great.

Franklin Roosevelt was a fighter. He fought, and for years, overcame Polio. He also was among the first to see the threat of Facism in Germany and Japan. Roosevelt was a leader at a time when people of all political parties were willing to fight to defend America and freedom.

TRUMAN also saw the threats facing our country. He was the first to step up in the fight against communism even when the nation was sick of war.

JFK was inspiration,

PENLEY

challenge, and dignity.

Camelot was backyard football and sailboats, pearls and state dinners. It was young but mature. It was an American vision. The sixties cried out for personalities and images to fill television sets, hearts and minds. Camelot bridged the divide between a nation still maintained by hopeful patriots, and a tumultuous

era dominated by protest and

cynicism.

"An intellectual is a man who takes more words than necessary to tell more than he knows."

Dwight D. Eisenhower

IKE was a calming voice of reason. He came from a poor family and rose to become supreme allied commander and then President.

PENLEY

Few presidents dreamed
as big as Reagan. He was
the eternal optimist. He
believed that "a rising tide
lifts all boats." He believed
in America. Reagan told the
story of some protesters
who came to his office.

"So they came in and, as was
the custom of the day, they were
barefoot with torn T-shirts,
and slouched in their chairs. And
finally one of them said to me
'Governor, it's impossible for you
to understand us... Your generation
didn't grow up in the era of space
travel, of jet travel, of cybernetics,
computers figuring in seconds what it
used to take men years to figure out."
Reagan told his white house audience
that he finally interrupted the student
saying "wait a minute. It's true what you
said. We didn't grow up with
those things. We invented them."

Reagan made us believe

in ourselves again.

America is a safe harbor for dreamers and the oppressed. It is an idea that burns in the soul of all good men. The proof can be found in the words of our founders:

"We hold these truths to be self-evident, that all men are created equal, that they are endowed by their creator with certain unalienable rights, that among these are life, liberty, and the pursuit of happiness."

PENLEY

The ideas of our founders were so rooted in truth that they were self-evident. God creates all men equal and no state can withhold those rights. Our founders' dreams would not be realized until much later in American History, but they would be realized. In this country all men have a chance to realize those dreams.

The western resonates with
so many Americans because
we all love the simple idea
of the tough but outnumbered
hero killing the bad guys.
Many of us hope that we
have a little bit of John
Wayne inside ourselves. Many
of our foreign friends have
called some of our leaders
"cowboys" as if that were
a bad thing to be. I can't
think of a greater compliment.

PENLEY

When I become president
I will be honored to be called
a cowboy. I'll even wear a
10 gallon hat and cowboy
boots just to antagonize
"them". The west captures
the adventurers spirit
of America. The cowboy is
symbolic of the type of
man that helped make
America great.

STARS of the
American Cinema are
familiar around the
world. For good or
for bad they are a
part of the face of
America. Even though
there is a dark side
to Hollywood it still
seems to reflect a
feeling of fun and
adventure that can
only be made in America.

PENLEY

Hollywood is part of the American dream. In the movies anything is possible.

PENLEY

Jimi Hendrix squeezed every ounce of American sweat from his Stratocaster. His version of our national Anthem is world renowned.

He seemed to bring every note to life. Even steeped in the cynical counter-culture of the day, he was breathing in the residual freedoms of expression left by our nations founders.

Americans remade music.
American culture reaches
every part of the globe
through our music. American
music is the best music.

It is in seeing an Andy Warhol Painting or listening to Bob Dylan or reading Mark Twain that we can appreciate the American character. These works are at once egalitarian, yet they reflect the exceptionalism of America. Elvis Presley came from nothing to become possibly the greatest music Icon of All time. He blended the music of several different cultures to create a uniquely American sound.

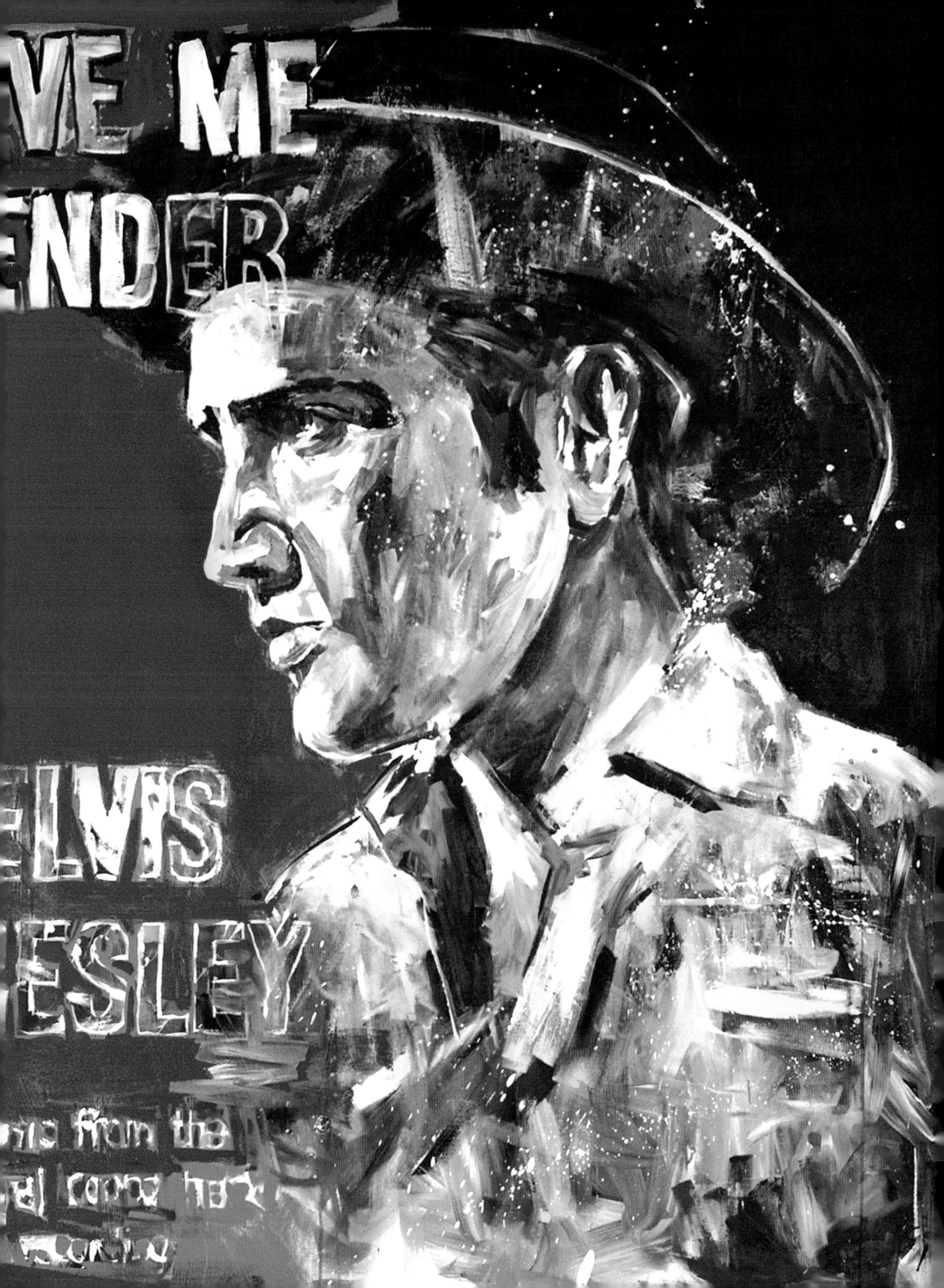
VE ME
NDER
ELVIS
ESLEY
from the

America invented, and
keeps reinventing,
Rock + Roll.

our music is so
good that you
don't have to be
able to understand
the words.

Even the poorest Americans are able to realize their dreams. Just as Elvis did, Johnny Cash rose above his humble start to become world famous. Only Americans can create music with such a unique sound. These men reflect the ingenuity of America in their music.

Americans recreate everything they do. We take music and make it our own. We take literature and make it our own. Some cultures never show significant change even after centuries, but America is constantly reinventing itself.

Whether from the depths
of the South or from the
streets of New York, all
of our different dialects,
traditions and Art somehow
combine to become
unquestionably American.
All of this creativity
reveals an American
flavor, an American
individualism.

Art and literature reflect the soul of a nation; Ours reflects a refusal to be ordinary. We have a need to be different and break new ground.

Whether they know it or not, our artists mirror the individual achievement mentality of our nation. The goodness of America is engrained in us all.

Why do we love sports the way we do. Just as we have done in the arts, we have recreated sports. Our sports are more than games. Our sports project uniquely American values. College football rivalries are reflections of our pride and loyalty for our friends and homes. Sports are reflections of our love of competition which makes America great.

Americans love achievement and sports are one of the best ways to see this. American universities build rivalries that help us exercise our need for competition. These players become legends and part of our folklore.

Sports touch a nostalgic chord and can bring back memories of past good times. Our heroes like Babe Ruth inspire all of us with their level of achievement. These sports heroes that we love transcend their sports; they are characters that we love for the images they became. When we think of Ali we think of the flash and depth of personality he possessed.

America loves an underdog because it takes us back to our roots. We are all underdogs at heart.

Bobby Jones personifies everything we want a sportsman to be. He was a Gentleman.

Our sports heroes seem invincible. We live vicariously through them, and maybe some of that invicibility is a part of us as a nation.

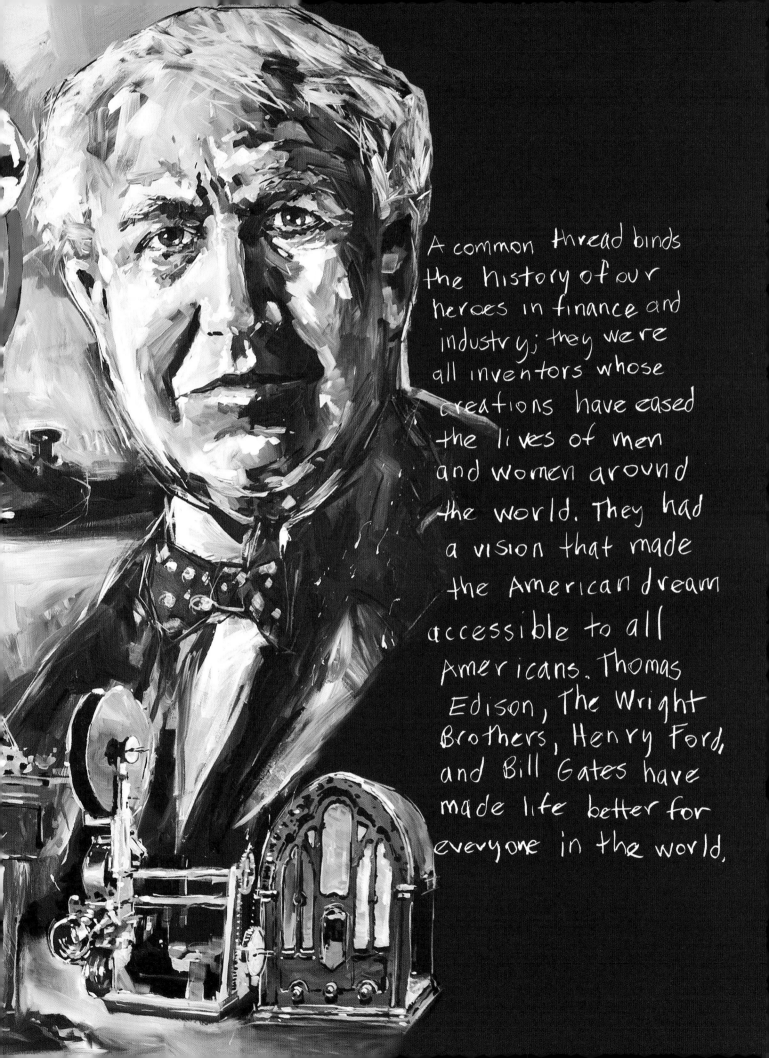

A common thread binds the history of our heroes in finance and industry; they were all inventors whose creations have eased the lives of men and women around the world. They had a vision that made the American dream accessible to all Americans. Thomas Edison, The Wright Brothers, Henry Ford, and Bill Gates have made life better for everyone in the world.

Why do we demonize industry? Maybe we should spend a few days in a pre-industrial world and then re-evaluate.

Wall Street was the birthplace of our government.

It is the capitol of capitalism.

Henry Ford made travel by car available to the common man. The automobile made America a little smaller.

where would the world be without America. Our critics need to Imagine a world without us to protect them. what power would rise to the top. I doubt that our critics would be happy about the alternatives. We are the good guys.

The intellectuals of Europe could not be so vocal without us to defend them against dictators.

They should realize that
A weak America is the
world's worst nightmare.

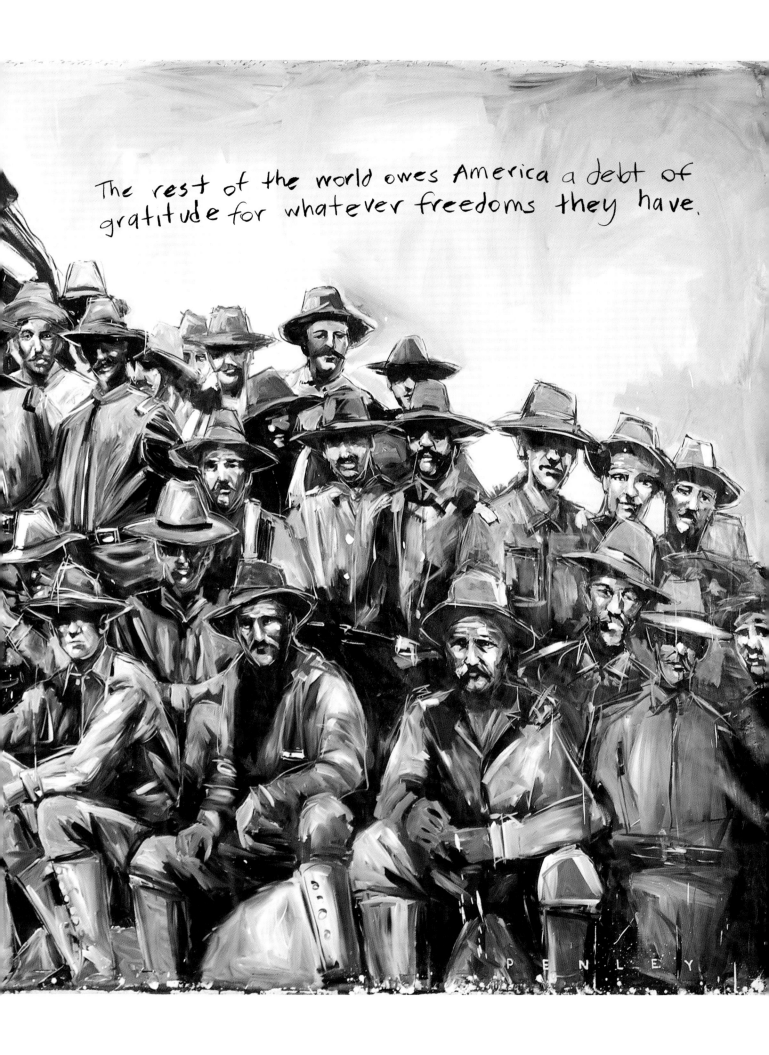

The places where we honor
the great men of our past
are hallowed ground to
Americans.

FROM THE MONUMENTS IN WASHINGTON
TO THE LIBERTY BELL IN PHILADELPHIA,
TO THE BATTLEFIELDS OF BOSTON,

THESE ARE THE AMERICAN MOMENTS
WHICH TIE US TOGETHER

Baseball, Football,
Hot dogs and Hamburgers,
Pick up trucks and Coke
bottles are all objects
that symbolize America.
These objects are Icons
of American culture
which give us a distinct
character. These things
evoke feelings of good
times which we can
remember even through
the hard times. They
are comforting.

Coca-Cola is the world's greatest brand. It is an ambassador of goodwill to the whole world.

Coke is a symbol of freedom and prosperity around the globe. The coke bottle is part of the brand of America. Coke is a symbol of the greatness of America.

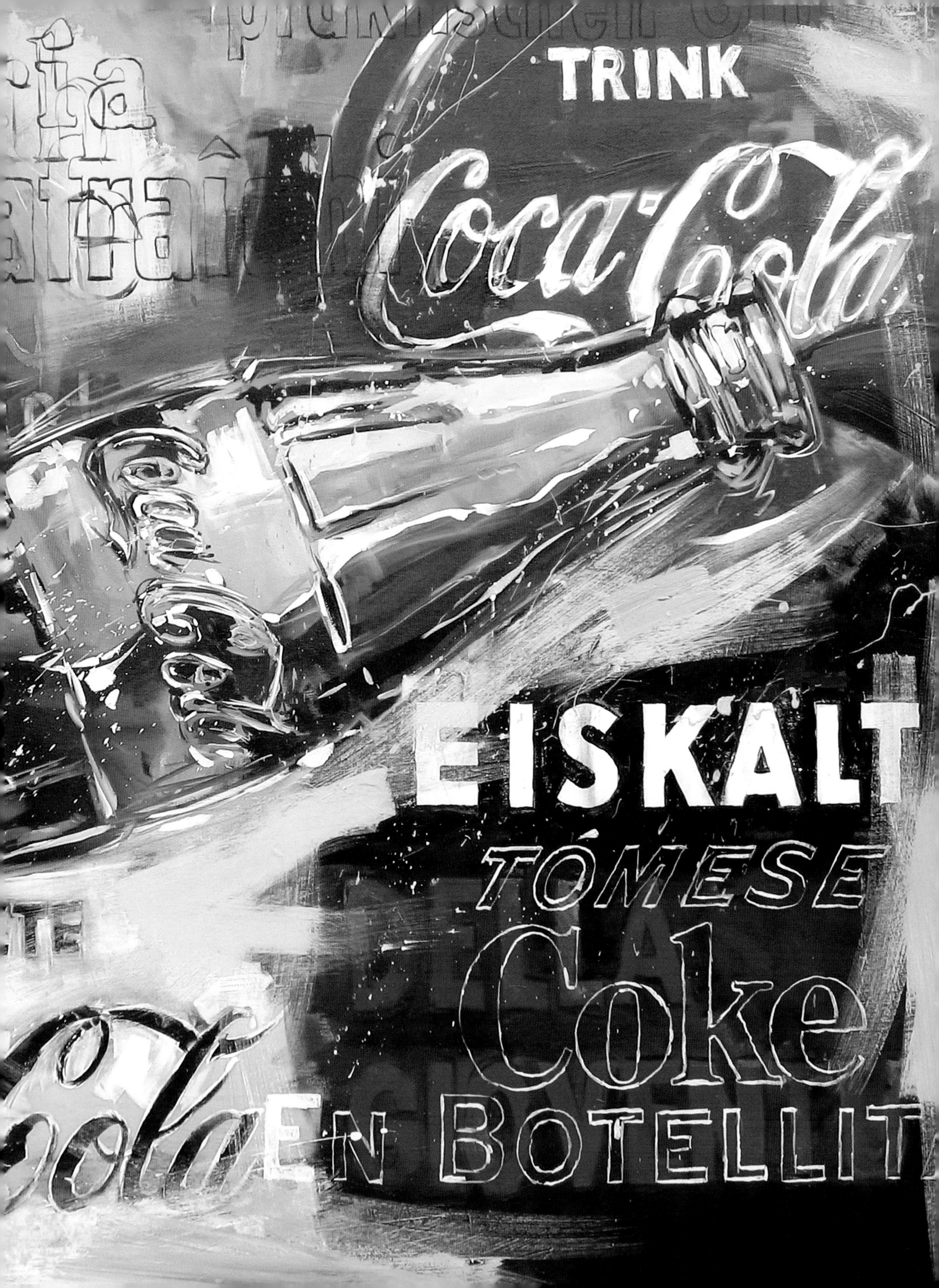
TRINK
Coca-Cola
EISKALT
TÓMESE
Coke
EN BOTELLIT

The list of contributions that the United States has made to the world cannot be measured. We provide basic necessities which help keep children alive and healthy all over the world. From Agriculture to medicine, we have given greatly to the quality of human life, Americans have followed their individual dreams and in doing so have made the world a better place. We sent men to the moon and in doing so discovered new technologies which have helped all the world. Capitalism has given men and women the incentive to create for the good of Americans and everyone else. Without America the world would be a very dark place. America is that shining city on a hill that Reagan dreamed of.

To the rest of the world
that might like to bash
America, or even those
malcontents here at
home I can only say,
show me a better place.

God Bless America.

Thanks so much to everyone who helped on this project. And especially to my editor Matt Carrothers, who was very patient in the process. To Neil Cavuto—I'm so honored that you would take the time from your busy schedule to support my effort in the reconstruction of America. To Ericka Pertierra, who somehow continues to answer my phone calls asking for big favors and assistance. Thanks, Bob, for not answering the phone. To Burtch Hunter—best book designer in the country, and to Libby for letting me ruin their vacation. To Dick Parker, for your help and support. To Rob Matre and Tim McClain—for their photography and support over the years. To Carole and Patrick Malloy—for friendship and partnership in this project along with some proofreading. To Herman Cain—without your help this book would not have come to fruition. To Brad Barfield—thank you for your brilliant sports analysis. To Saxby Chambliss—thank you for participating in the project. To Della Wells—thank you for your proofreading. To Mercer University Press— for taking on a project with an artist who was voted mostly likely not to receive a Pulitzer Prize. To my parents for indulging me in my art habits. Finally, to my beautiful wife Carrie, for being patient and living with me somehow every day.